**W9-AEA-629**

DISCARDED

Nashua Public Library

Enjoy this book!
Please remember to return it on time
so that others may enjoy it too.

Manage your library account and
discover all we offer by visiting us
online at www.nashualibrary.org

Love your library? Tell a friend!

J

ENGINEERING
THE LEANING TOWER OF PISA

BY ADAM FURGANG

CONTENT CONSULTANT
Antonio Nanni, PhD, PE
Professor, University of Miami

Core Library

An Imprint of Abdo Publishing
abdopublishing.com

Cover image: For more than 800 years, the Leaning
Tower of Pisa has had its signature tilt.

abdopublishing.com

Published by Abdo Publishing, a division of ABDO, PO Box 398166,
Minneapolis, Minnesota 55439. Copyright © 2018 by Abdo Consulting
Group, Inc. International copyrights reserved in all countries. No part of this
book may be reproduced in any form without written permission from the
publisher. Core Library™ is a trademark and logo of Abdo Publishing.

Printed in the United States of America, North Mankato, Minnesota
102017
012018

THIS BOOK CONTAINS
RECYCLED MATERIALS

Cover Photo: Shutterstock Images
Interior Photos: Shutterstock Images, 1, 15; Catarina Belova/Shutterstock Images, 4–5, 43;
Evgeny Shmulev/Shutterstock Images, 7; Ross Helen/Shutterstock Images, 10; Giulio Napolitani/
AFP/Getty Images, 12–13; Antonio Gravante/Shutterstock Images, 16–17; Simon Montgomery/
robertharding/Getty Images, 20; Fredrik Von Erichsen/picture alliance/dpa/Newscom, 22–23, 45;
Fedor Selivanov/Shutterstock Images, 25; S. Borisov/Shutterstock Images, 27 (left); Sergey Dzyuba/
Shutterstock Images, 27 (middle); Radoslaw Maciejewski/Shutterstock Images, 27 (right); Fabio
Muzzi/AP Images, 30–31, 38, 40; Red Line Editorial, 32; Alberto Bernasconi/Bloomberg/Getty
Images, 35; Giulio Andreini/Liaison/Hulton Archive/Getty Images, 37

Editor: Arnold Ringstad
Imprint Designer: Maggie Villaume
Series Design Direction: Laura Polzin

Publisher's Cataloging-in-Publication Data

Names: Furgang, Adam, author.
Title: Engineering the Leaning Tower of Pisa / by Adam Furgang.
Description: Minneapolis, Minnesota : Abdo Publishing, 2018. | Series: Building by design |
        Includes online resources and index.
Identifiers: LCCN 2017946938 | ISBN 9781532113734 (lib.bdg.) | ISBN 9781532152610
        (ebook)
Subjects: LCSH: Leaning Tower (Pisa, Italy)--Juvenile literature. | Architecture,
        Romanesque—Juvenile literature. | Christian art and symbolism--Medieval,
        500-1500--Juvenile literature. | Building--Juvenile literature.
Classification: DDC 725.9709--dc23
LC record available at https://lccn.loc.gov/2017946938

CONTENTS

CHAPTER ONE
A Leaning Tower 4

CHAPTER TWO
Preparing to Build. 12

CHAPTER THREE
Building the Tower 22

CHAPTER FOUR
The Tower Today 30

Fast Facts 42

Stop and Think 44

Glossary 46

Online Resources 47

Learn More 47

Index 48

About the Author 48

A LEANING TOWER

I n some ways, the Leaning Tower of Pisa is an architectural failure. In other ways, it is an engineering wonder. Builders normally want to make structures as sturdy and safe as possible. Buildings are meant to be strong, straight, and made to last. However, this is not what happened with the world-famous Tower of Pisa in Pisa, Italy. Poor planning and soft ground worked against this amazing bell tower. These factors caused a tilt in the structure that was never meant to happen. Over time, the tower came to lean about 5.5 degrees

The leaning tower is one part of a larger complex in Pisa.

from vertical. Now the tower is known more for its tilt than for anything else.

The Leaning Tower of Pisa is called Torre Pendente di Pisa in Italy. It is in northwestern Tuscany, in the country's central region. The tower is found in the walled Piazza dei Miracoli. This area's name means "square of miracles." The tower is one of several buildings that make up the church grounds there. The others include the baptistery and the cathedral. The Piazza dei Miracoli is also called the Piazza del Duomo. In Italian the word *duomo* means "cathedral."

Construction started on the tower on August 9, 1173. No one wanted the tower to tilt or lean. A leaning tower could possibly fall over. It would have been an embarrassment. But the tower was built near the sea. It was on soft, silty soil. Because the tower is made of marble, it is very heavy and sank into this soil.

The cathedral is surrounded by a large grassy space.

THE TOWER TELLS A STORY

The Leaning Tower of Pisa has been through a lot. It took almost 200 years to complete. It was not finished until 1372. Some of the long breaks in construction were because of wars. For centuries after it was done, its tilt slowly worsened. In recent decades, engineers have worked to save the tower from the disaster of collapsing.

The tower is now a tourist attraction. Every year more than 6 million people visit the city of Pisa. They want to see the Piazza

THINK ABOUT THE SOIL

The type of soil upon which a building stands is important. Some kinds of soil are softer than others. Some soils have a lot of clay and sand in them. This silty soil contains small particles. Other soils have a lot of gravel in them. Gravelly soil contains large particles. The best soils are those that do not change shape under a building's weight. This will keep the structure from shifting or leaning. Today builders know a lot more about soil than they did in the past. They can make the ground safe before building.

dei Miracoli and its tilted tower. Pisa relies on the money tourists spend there when they visit.

In the 1990s, the tower had to close to the public for many years. Engineers were worried that it could fall over. If that happened, people could get hurt or killed. A collapse would also harm the area's tourism industry. The work to keep the tower from falling over was not easy. It took many years of engineering and modern technology. In 2001 the tower reopened. The tilt was lessened and the tower was stabilized. However, engineers did not correct the tilt entirely. The Leaning Tower of Pisa continues

The tower is a popular spot for tourist photos.

to lean slightly. Today the tower keeps amazing new generations of visitors. Everyone wants to see its unique lean and the beauty of its architecture.

STRAIGHT TO THE
SOURCE

In 1999 the television program *NOVA* interviewed Piero Pierotti, a historian at Pisa University. He described the importance of the Tower of Pisa at the time it was built:

> It's said that the most important families in Pisa ate off gold plates, so there's no doubt that some had grown very rich from seagoing trade. And this wealth must have inspired the attempt to do something outstanding for the city.
>
> While all the other monuments of the Piazza have been signed by their architects, the architect of the Tower is a mystery. Nobody put their name on the Tower. The builders must have felt that the plan for the Tower was over-ambitious, because they knew that the ground in Pisa tended to give way easily.

Source: "Fall of the Leaning Tower." *NOVA*. PBS, October 5, 1999. Web. Accessed August 8, 2017.

What's the Big Idea?

What is one of the main ideas in Piero Pierotti's quote? Name two details that support this idea.

CHAPTER
TWO

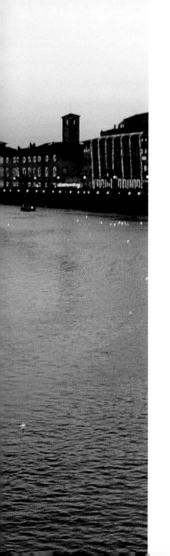

PREPARING TO BUILD

The name *Pisa* comes from a Greek word meaning "marshy land." The city of Pisa was built very close to the Ligurian Sea. This is a portion of the larger Mediterranean Sea. As a result of this location, some of the city's buildings began to sink into the soft soil. The Leaning Tower is the most famous example of this.

From its very beginning, Pisa's seaside location had helped it gain power. In the year 180 BCE, the city of Pisa was a Roman colony called Colonia Julia Pisana. When the Romans controlled the area, they used the

The Arno River runs through Pisa and into the Mediterranean Sea just a few miles away.

DIGGING DEEP TO BUILD HIGH

Today engineers can safely build skyscrapers on soft ground. They place poles called piles, made of steel, concrete, or timber, deep into the ground as part of the building's foundation. This makes the building more stable. One example of this can be seen in the Shanghai Tower in Shanghai, China. This tower opened in 2014. It stands 2,073 feet (632 m) tall. Like the Leaning Tower of Pisa, there is soft soil in the area. Builders drove 980 piles into the ground. Some were as deep as 282 feet (86 m). Then they poured 2.15 million cubic feet (61,000 cubic m) of concrete to create a thick, heavy base for the skyscraper.

city as a base for army ships. They did this because the sea was much closer to the city then. Pisa used to be located right next to the Ligurian Sea. The city did not move over time. But the shoreline did. Over the centuries, sand and silt running out from the Arno River added more land. The shoreline slowly separated the city from the sea. Today the city of Pisa sits farther back from the sea than ever before.

The tower's base is sturdy enough to support the structure, but the soil below is not.

The Piazza dei Miracoli, with its beautiful marble architecture, is considered sacred by the Catholic Church.

For many hundreds of years, war and fighting were common in and around Pisa. Between the years 300 and 1011 CE, barbarians, Vikings, and Saracens all fought with Pisa. By 1063 Pisa was very wealthy from its sea trading. Some of those riches were used to build the Piazza dei Miracoli and the cathedral.

Soft ground by the sea is mostly made up of sand, mud, and clay. From the beginning, builders in Pisa knew the ground was not ideal. However, steps were taken to make the tower as stable as possible. Building a round structure was one helpful plan. Round structures are more stable than rectangular ones. Having a circular base means the structure is equally stable in all directions.

Making impressive buildings was very common in Italy during this period. Large towers were status symbols among different families and regions. Competition to make the tallest tower was happening around Italy at the time.

The building style of the tower was called Pisan Romanesque. It used colonnades, or columns, along with arches. Using columns and arches meant the tower wouldn't need as much additional reinforcement.

FITTING IN WITH THE CATHEDRAL

The era in which the Piazza del Duomo was built was called the Middle Ages, or Medieval Period. This era lasted from the 400s CE to the 1400s. In 1118 Pope Gelasius II consecrated, or dedicated, the cathedral. The cathedral was still unfinished at the time. By that time even the building's architect, Buscheto, had died. Buscheto was buried next to the building.

The bell tower was an afterthought for the cathedral grounds. It was not planned until well after the cathedral and baptistery were underway. The tall tower was meant to be a final touch to the square. Its grand height and fancy design would show off the other structures.

The Tower of Pisa would have a marble staircase. The design was meant to demonstrate the status of the city of Pisa. However, marble is heavy. The extra weight on the soft soil was a bad combination.

The soft subsoil put all the building

projects in peril long before work even began. The tower would soon begin to sink and lean. The cathedral and the baptistery suffered from the same problem. The heavy white marble on all three structures was one factor causing them to sink.

FURTHER EVIDENCE

Chapter Two discusses many details about the building of the Leaning Tower of Pisa. Visit the website below to read more about the structure. Does the information on the website support what you learned in Chapter Two? What new information did you learn from the website?

WHY DOES THE LEANING TOWER OF PISA LEAN?
abdocorelibrary.com/engineering-leaning-tower-of-pisa

The tower's marble staircase contributes to its great weight.

BUILDING THE TOWER

In the 1100s and 1200s, there were hundreds of bell towers throughout Italy. The Piazza dei Miracoli would not be complete without one. In 1172 an Italian widow named Berta di Bernardo set aside 60 gold coins in her will. They were meant for buying stones to begin construction on the bell tower. When she died, the coins were given to a group of builders. They were in charge of finding stones. For at least a year before building began, the men went back and forth to San Giuliano, Italy. They slowly gathered all the stones they needed. Finally they were

Bell towers were important parts of many Italian communities in the Middle Ages.

SKILLED MASONS

Many artists and craftspeople worked on the Leaning Tower of Pisa. However, it was the masons who were the most important to the construction. A mason is someone who works with stones, bricks, and mortar. Masons selected special types of stone from quarries. Then they cut off large blocks from the stones. From these they sculpted smaller blocks for the columns and other sections. The masons who worked on the tower were not ordinary working peasants. They were some of the most skilled craftsmen in the world. Many had traveled to other regions and were able to include some of the latest influences and techniques of the time.

ready to get started on the tower.

At the time, it was not common to use columns and arches to support a building's weight. The process required many skilled builders and craftsman. Many masons, stonecutters, and sculptors worked on the tower. Each element was complex. They had to work together to get the job done.

The building's lean was already becoming clear after just a few levels were completed.

200 YEARS IN THE MAKING

The original builders of the tower knew about the soft ground in the region. However, they did not plan well enough. A hole only about five feet (1.5 m) deep was dug into the ground's soft clay and sand. The idea was to remove soil that would change shape. But the depth was not nearly enough for the tower's weight.

Work on the tower did not happen quickly. The first building phase ran from 1173 until 1178. During that time, only three stories were finished. The building began to develop a slight lean. Construction stopped for nearly a century. The weight of the three floors created pressure on the ground. This allowed the soil to settle over time. It compacted and made the ground more stable. Historians believe that the long break is what kept the tower from falling in later centuries. Stopping construction may have saved the building.

In 1272 work on the bell tower resumed. Architect Giovanni di Simone became the new architect when construction began again. Four more floors were added to the tower. The tower continued to lean on its small, shallow foundation. The soil on one side of the base changed shape more than the soil on the other side.

COMPARING
LEANS

The Leaning Tower of Pisa is not the only landmark that leans. What is the difference in leans between the Leaning Tower of Pisa and the other landmarks shown?

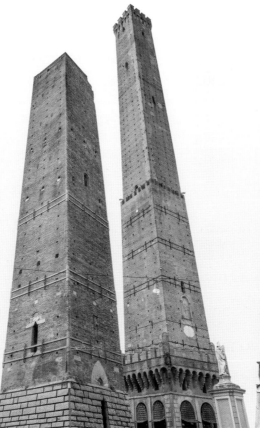

ELIZABETH TOWER, UNITED KINGDOM. LEAN: 0.28°

TOWERS OF BOLOGNA, ITALY. LEAN: 4° (LEFT TOWER), 1.3° (RIGHT TOWER)

LEANING TOWER OF PISA, ITALY. LEAN: 4.95°

A LEGEND OF THE TOWER

Scientist Galileo Galilei was born in the town of Pisa in 1589. Popular stories claim that Galileo performed one of his most famous experiments at the tower. He dropped two spheres of different masses from the top level. He wanted to test how long it took the items to reach the ground. For example, would a large rock reach the ground faster than a small pebble because it is heavier? His experiment showed that mass does not affect how long it takes an object to reach the ground. This was an important idea. Most historians believe the experiment did not happen as described, though the story has become a major part of the tower's legacy.

This issue got worse over time. To make up for the lean, the new floors were angled to straighten out the tower. Because of this, the tower is not built completely straight. It leans in one direction and curves slightly in the other direction. Construction halted again in 1278.

Architect Tommaso di Andrea Pisano completed the tower in 1372. It had a section at the top called a bell chamber. This is the area where the large bells are held. Within the bell chamber, several heavy bells were added. Each bell rings as a musical note on a major scale. The biggest bell was put in the tower in 1655. The extra weight of the bells added to the building's tilt. By the time it was complete, the tower weighed 16,000 tons (14,500 metric tons).

EXPLORE ONLINE

Chapter Three discusses the work that went into building the famous Tower of Pisa. But it is not the only building in the world that leans. Visit the website below to learn about other leaning towers. How is the information similar to what you learned in Chapter Three? How is it different? What new details did you learn about why buildings lean?

TILTED TOWERS: THE SECRETS BENEATH THE WORLD'S LEANING BUILDINGS
abdocorelibrary.com/engineering-leaning-tower-of-pisa

CHAPTER
FOUR

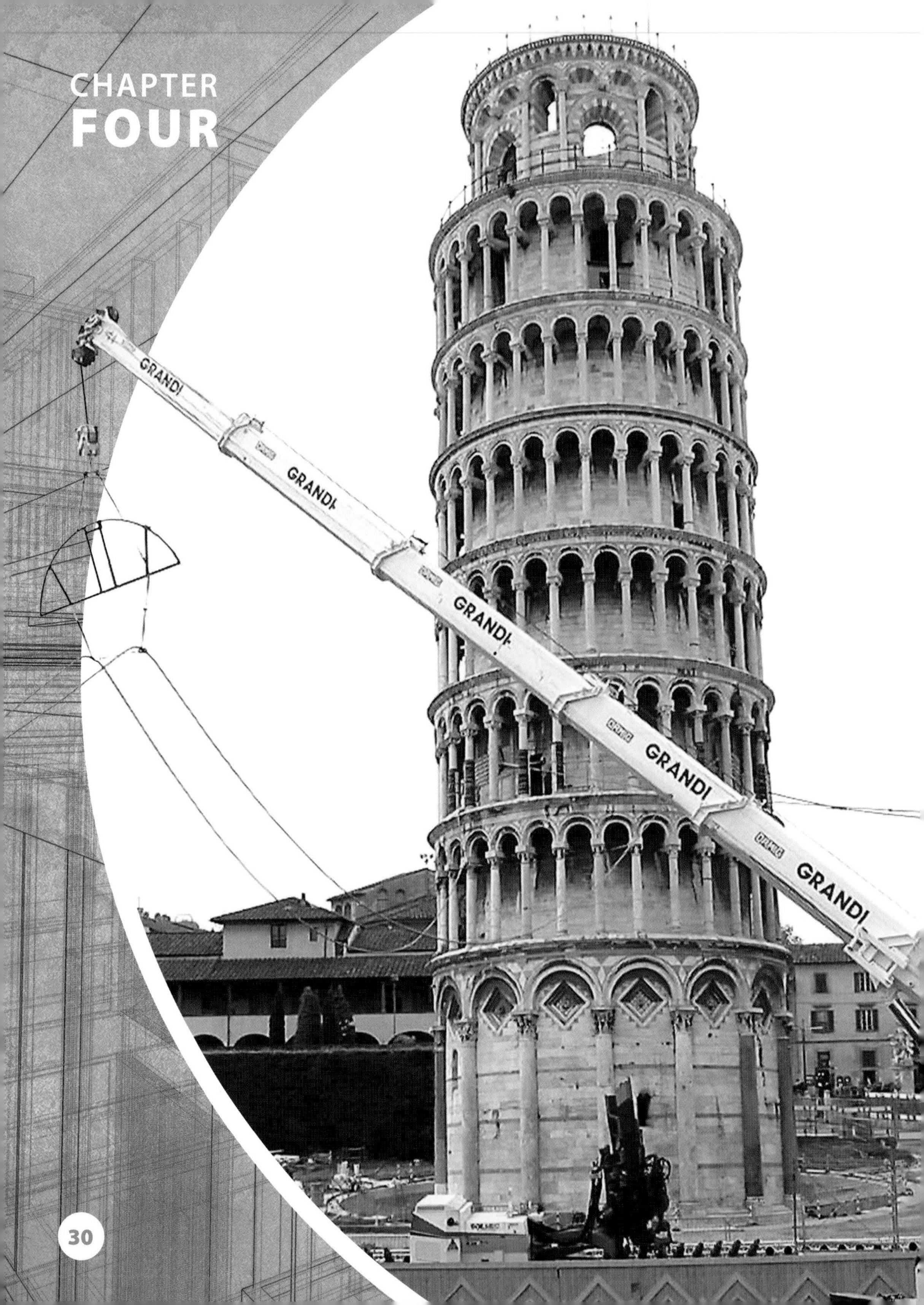

THE TOWER TODAY

How can a leaning tower be fixed? Efforts to adjust the crooked bell tower have been made for hundreds of years. Engineers, scientists, and government leaders have all given their opinions about the problem.

By the 1900s, the Leaning of Tower of Pisa had become famous around the world for its tilt. Because the tower continued to tilt more and more over time, engineers feared it could collapse. That would be very dangerous. It would also mean the loss of a famous landmark. In 1911, the Italian government started taking measurements

Stabilizing the Leaning Tower of Pisa has been a major engineering challenge.

CONSTRUCTION
TIMELINE

The Leaning Tower of Pisa was completed over the course of several hundred years. This timeline shows some of the key dates in this process. How would such a long building schedule affect a project? What additional challenges would it create? Would it bring any advantages?

1655
The largest bell is added.

1371
The tower is completed.

1272–1278
Work resumes.

1173–1178
The first building phase occurs.

1172
Berta di Bernardo provides money for construction.

of the tilt. The records would track how far the tower was leaning. They could track changes in the leaning. Engineers learned the tower was tipping to the south by about one twentieth of an inch (0.13 cm) every year. At its top, it was leaning more than 13 feet (4 m) from a straight position.

Italian dictator Benito Mussolini thought the tower was a national embarrassment. He tried to fix the problem. In 1934 hundreds of holes were drilled into the base. Eighty tons (73 metric tons) of cement were injected into the holes. This was meant to make the

WORLD WAR II

During World War II (1939–1945), it is possible that the Leaning Tower of Pisa was used as a lookout. Lookout towers were thought of as a threat during the war. A sniper could sit in a tall tower and shoot at soldiers on the ground. US military officials considered destroying the Leaning Tower of Pisa. But when the US troops arrived, they found the entire area to be so impressive that they left the tower standing. The building survived the war without damage.

TAKING ON THE TOWER

In 1990 a special commission was put together to fix the tower and make it safe for the public. The commission was led by John Burland. He is an engineer who is an expert in soil. He understood that the tower was not meant to be straightened. It was just meant to be safe for the public. "No one need worry that the tower is going to end up straight," he said. "That is one of two unacceptable results. The other we don't dare mention."

ground more stable. But it only made things worse. The extra weight on the base made the tower even more unstable. The tower tilted farther.

In the 1980s, new concern and attention were given to the tower's safety. On March 17, 1989, the Civic Tower in Pavia, Italy, collapsed without warning. The Civic Tower was not leaning. There were no visible signs that the building was weak. Four people were killed, and more than a dozen were injured. In response to that sudden collapse, the Leaning Tower of Pisa was closed to visitors in 1990.

Engineers sought to keep the tower's lean while making it safe. This would maintain the tower's iconic look and help tourism.

Engineers became more worried than ever about the structure. Urgent attention was given to correcting the tilt. By this time, the tower was leaning at 5.5 degrees. Its top was 17 feet (5.2 m) from a vertical position.

In 1992 sensors were installed. They keep track of the slightest movement of the tower or ground.

They also track movements in cracks already in the building. Wire sensors and devices called inclinometers were also added. They measure any tilting or shifting of the building. In July of 1993, 600 tons (544 metric tons) of lead weights were placed at the base of the north side of the tower to offset the uneven soil. This would prevent the lean from getting worse. The lead weights helped correct the lean by about one inch (2.54 cm).

Another effort was made in 1995. The idea was to freeze the ground around the tower. This was done so that cables could be driven under the ground to make the tower more stable. A substance called liquid nitrogen was used for the job. It helps freeze objects quickly. This effort did not work well. The tower's tilt became worse overnight, and the effort was stopped. More lead weights were added.

A technician checks some of the 41 drills used to stabilize the tower between 1999 and 2001.

THE TOWER TODAY

Engineers were not trying to straighten the tower completely. They wanted to preserve some of its famous tilt. But a correction to a safer, more stable position was needed. Cables were attached to the tower in 1998. Their ends were anchored 100 yards (91 m) away. This released pressure at points of stress on the building. Then in June 1999, 41 special soil drills were inserted under the north side of the tower. The drills removed soil from the ground. Engineers hoped this would cause gravity to help correct the lean.

The soil drills removed 1,340 cubic feet (38 cubic m) of soil. Work ended in May 2001. The project was a success. The tower's lean was corrected by about 17 inches (43 cm). On December 15, 2001, the tower reopened to the public. Today the tower leans about 13.5 feet (4.1 m) from vertical and is said to be stable for the next few hundred years.

Making the tower safe required significant work at the site.

Tourists returned to the tower soon after its reopening.

The Leaning Tower of Pisa remains one of the most famous landmarks on Earth. Although it is known for a mistake in its construction, it continues to amaze visitors from all around the world. Modern technology and engineering will continue to preserve its legacy for centuries to come.

STRAIGHT TO THE
SOURCE

Civil engineer John Burland described the efforts to stop the tower's lean and make it safe:

The classic solutions involve what's called compensation grouting or injecting grouting into the ground to try and lift one side of the building compared to the other. It has to be carefully controlled and it uses very specialized equipment.

Or you can cut the building at its foundation level to insert jacks and jack the building straight, that has been done many times.

At Pisa, because the ground was so incredibly soft, we did the opposite and took some ground out.

But it's not something you rush into. . . . you can get it terribly wrong if you haven't got the techniques to do it properly.

Source: Georgia McCafferty. "Tilted Towers." *CNN*. CNN, March 2, 2017. Web. Accessed August 8, 2017.

Back It Up

What do you think the engineer meant by "you can get it terribly wrong"? What is at stake in a big engineering project like the one at the Leaning Tower of Pisa?

FAST FACTS

- The Leaning Tower of Pisa is part of the Piazza dei Miracoli in Pisa, Italy.

- The tower was built during the Middle Ages.

- Construction began in 1173, after a year of collecting the stones for the structure.

- Construction stopped after three stories were built.

- Work restarted on the building nearly 100 years later. This allowed soil to become more compact and made the tower a little more stable than it would have been without the pause in building.

- Work on the tower stopped again in 1278.

- When work began on the top section, the lean was visible. Workers attempted to fix the problem.

- Work on the tower was completed in about 1370.

- The largest of the seven bells was added in 1655. It weighs about 3.5 tons (3.2 metric tons).

- Italian dictator Benito Mussolini thought the Leaning Tower of Pisa was a national embarrassment.

- In 1934 Mussolini had mortar injected into the base. But instead of making the tower more stable, it made the lean even worse.

- In 1990 the tower was closed to the public so a restoration project could begin.

- The tower reopened to the public in 2001.

STOP AND
THINK

Tell the Tale

Chapter One discusses the planning for the Leaning Tower of Pisa. Imagine you are planning the tower during the Middle Ages. Write 200 words about how you envision the grand tower once it is finished.

Dig Deeper

Galileo Galilei is said to have performed a famous experiment off the top of the Leaning Tower of Pisa. With an adult's help, find out more about the experiment and about Galileo's life. Write a paragraph about what you learned.

Take a Stand

The Leaning Tower of Pisa is famous for its lean. Write a letter to critics who think the lean should be corrected rather than left alone. What reasons can you give to back up your argument?

Why Do I Care?

You may not have been to the Leaning Tower of Pisa. But you can still consider why it is important. Why do you think the Leaning Tower is so admired by tourists? How does the tower link us to the past? Think about what makes landmarks special to people all around the world.

GLOSSARY

architect
a person who designs buildings and oversees construction

baptistery
part of a church used for a religious ceremony called a baptism

colonnades
columns that support a roof

consecrate
to dedicate something in a religious ceremony

mortar
a mixture of cement, sand, and water used for bonding bricks or stones in a building process

nave
the center section of a church

silt
fine sand or clay deposited by running water

sniper
a person who shoots a gun from a hidden place, often from a high location

status symbols
things that indicate wealth or high position in society

ONLINE RESOURCES

To learn more about the Leaning Tower of Pisa, visit our free resource websites below.

Visit **abdocorelibrary.com** for free Common Core resources for teachers and students, including vetted activities, multimedia, and booklinks, for deeper subject comprehension.

Visit **abdobooklinks.com** for free additional online weblinks for further learning. These links are routinely monitored and updated to provide the most current information available.

LEARN MORE

Armstrong, Simon. *Cool Architecture: Filled with Fantastic Facts for Kids of All Ages*. London: Pavilion Books, 2015.

INDEX

Andrea Pisano,
  Tommaso di, 9, 28
architects, 9, 11, 18,
  26, 28
architecture, 18

bell tower, 19, 23, 26,
  28–29
Bernardo, Berta di,
  23, 32
builders, 9, 11, 23–25
Burland, John, 34, 41
Buscheto, 18–19

construction, 6, 8,
  23–26, 28, 32
craftspeople, 24

design, 19

engineers, 8–9, 14,
  31, 33–35, 39, 41

Galilei, Galileo, 28

maintenance, 35–36,
  39
marble, 6, 19, 21
Mussolini, Benito, 33

Piazza dei Miracoli, 6,
  8–9, 16
Piazza del Duomo, 6,
  18
Pierotti, Piero, 11
Pisa, Italy, 5, 8–9, 11,
  13–14, 16–17, 19
Pisano, Bonanno, 9
Pisano, Giovanni, 9

sensors, 35–36
Simone, Giovanni di,
  26
soil, 6, 8, 13, 19, 26,
  34, 36, 39
stability, 9, 14, 17–18,
  26, 31, 33–36, 39

tilt, 5–6, 8–9, 29, 31,
  34–36, 39
Tuscany, 6

About the Author

Adam Furgang's writing credits include more than a dozen nonfiction books in the middle school market about topics as diverse as nutrition, conservation, art, space, and engineering. He has a background in art, design, and photography, and he lives in upstate New York with his wife and two sons.